DIGITAL AND INFORMATION LITERACY ™

GAMIFICATION
USING GAMING TECHNOLOGY
FOR ACHIEVING GOALS

THERESE SHEA

rosen publishing's
rosen
central®

New York

Published in 2014 by The Rosen Publishing Group, Inc.
29 East 21st Street, New York, NY 10010

Copyright © 2014 by The Rosen Publishing Group, Inc.

First Edition

Library of Congress Cataloging-in-Publication Data

Shea, Therese.
Gamification: using gaming technology for achieving goals/Therese Shea.
    p. cm.—(Digital and information literacy)
Includes bibliographical references and index.
ISBN 978-1-4488-9512-0 (library binding: alk. paper)
1. Gambling. 2. Incentives in industry. 3. Incentives in conservation of natural resources. I. Title.
GV1301.S48 2014
795—dc23

2012036231

Manufactured in the United States of America

CPSIA Compliance Information: Batch #S13YA: For further information, contact Rosen Publishing, New York, New York, at 1-800-237-9932.

CONTENTS

INTRODUCTION

Do you remember your parents making ordinary chores fun? Perhaps you and your sister raced to see who could get dressed the quickest. Or you and your brother competed to see who could clean the best. Did the winner receive a treat? Doing something well is its own reward, but getting recognition or even a prize is another motivation to try harder to achieve a goal. Of course, if activities are fun, they are even easier to complete.

Yes, rewards and games are a big part of childhood, but what about now? Are older people rewarded for doing ordinary things? Are certain activities presented to them as games so that they will be more likely to participate? This happens more than people realize, especially with the increased use of technology in people's everyday lives.

Though a recent buzzword in today's culture, "gamification" is an old concept. It means applying game-related ideas to nongame processes, issues, and situations. The result is an engaging and gratifying experience for the participant. For example, LevelUp is an application for smartphones. It offers users incentives to visit certain restaurants and stores. Each time they go to these places, they are rewarded with coupons and other deals, like a digital customer loyalty program. Similarly, many credit cards offer consumer rewards programs. Accumulating a certain number of points can mean cash back or travel vouchers.

According to a Pew Internet Project survey, 25 percent of Americans use their smartphones instead of a computer. This behavior is partly why the gamification of technology is on the rise.

From these examples, commerce seems an obvious field for gamification. Gamelike activities can entice people to buy. But what about directing the concepts of gamification to other areas, specifically to issues that could improve lives and maybe even society in general? Could it work?

The car company Volkswagen invited the public to post ideas for a gamelike concept that could promote positive behavior. One man suggested using cameras to take photographs of cars driving at a proper speed, rather than speeding cars. All law-abiding drivers could be placed in a lottery with the chosen winner receiving money collected from the fines of speeding drivers. Not only does this idea add a fun incentive to maintain a proper speed on roadways, but it actually works. A three-day demonstration on a busy city street in Sweden showed a drop in average speed. This is an example of the gamification of street traffic.

Some enterprising people have applied similar outside-the-box thinking to issues involving the environment, education, health and medicine, global conflicts, and other matters. Video games and mobile applications are a major part of gamification. However, as with the speed-camera project, gamifying can manifest itself in simpler, nondigital contexts. The object of gamification, however, is unwavering: to make serious goals more fun, achievable, and rewarding. This book highlights some of the most surprising, creative, and popular applications of gamification. They encompass many attributes of today's gamification movement.

Chapter 1

Gaming on the Rise

According to the *Economist*, the PricewaterhouseCoopers consulting firm reported that the gaming industry would soon reach nearly $100 billion. One reason for the industry's success is that video games are no longer just a pastime for young people. A study by the U.S. Entertainment Software Association (ESA) found that the average gamer is thirty-seven years old. Also, about 42 percent of all gamers are female. What this means for gamification is that a growing population enjoys the kind of interaction and challenges that games, specifically video and digital games, provide.

What Makes a Game Fun?

Many games and kinds of games are available today. Why do some board games, card games, video games, and Web applications seem more fun than others? Some game developers study games in an attempt to determine why some are more successful than others. Great graphics and a cool soundtrack are helpful, but there is more to it. Here are some characteristics of a good game. Not all games have every one of these characteristics, but many of the most profitable and popular do.

Some treadmills use gamification features in their software that challenge runners to complete certain milestones.

Challenging, Achievable Goals

A game should be continuously challenging but achievable. If it is too difficult, the player may give up too soon. If the challenge is too easy, players may tire of it or perhaps only play it once. A game should have short- and long-term goals. When each short-term goal is met, the next should interest the players enough to keep them moving toward an ultimate goal. The best games also allow for more than one way to achieve a goal.

File   Edit   View   Favorites   Tools   Help

GAMIFYING THE WORKPLACE

Gamifying the Workplace

Few people think going to work is like a game, which makes it an appropriate environment to spice up with gamification. Gamification lends itself to certain workplaces, such as those at which employees sell products. However, it can be applied to other kinds of work and work processes as well. For example, learning new computer applications could earn an employee points that can be cashed in for a day off. Rewards, acknowledgements, and other incentives are motivations for employees beyond a paycheck.

Many work environments offer an annual review and, depending on effort, a salary increase. An ongoing game might allow managers and workers to monitor progress more often than that. Gamification can make workplace achievements more public, too. Employees can track their own progress and that of others to ensure a consistently high-effort workforce. When certain employees are identified as being at the top of their field, their method of getting to the top could be examined and perhaps implemented for other employees to follow.

Workplaces can be stressful environments. Gamifying everyday tasks is one way to acknowledge and reward workers for their efforts.

An Interesting Storyline or World

A game is more engaging if it has a storyline or at least presents an inter-esting world to "live in" for a while. This draws the player into the game and helps users identify with their quest. A good mix of reality and fantasy helps players know what to expect based on their own experiences and yet escape from their own reality, too.

Rewards Beyond Just Winning

A game seems more interesting if it has a system of rewards. Rather than simply focusing on the end point—winning the game—the user can find the experience of the game itself rewarding enough to want to stay and explore. A player will also want to keep playing if he or she feels a sense of satisfac-tion or value in the activity.

Bunchball is a major developer of gamification platforms for businesses. Currently, Bunchball is tracking 125 million users, including Warner Bros., Comcast, NBC Universal, and ABC Television. Bunchball chief executive officer Jim Scullion explained his company's success to *Forbes*, "Whenever performing an activity consistently to a high standard is crucial to business success, gamification can help. That's why CEOs should be interested. Gamification is an excellent way to effect and sustain change."

Mobile Games

The advent of mobile technology made gaming-on-the-go a standard in devices such as smartphones and digital tablets. (The ESA study notes that 55 percent of gamers play on their phones or other handheld devices.) Mobile games are now a common way to pass the time at the bus stop and to keep in touch with friends. Social networking sites such as Facebook host social games, such as Zynga's addictive and user-friendly simulation FarmVille. Users create and maintain a successful farm and interact with Facebook friends. Certain items within the game can be purchased using

Bunchball vice president Gary Chavez explains new ways that entertainment and gaming applications can be moneymakers for businesses.

virtual cash or actual money. FarmVille mastered several points of the good game formula. It is an engaging world, achievable but challenging, and has a complex reward system. Another mobile application, Foursquare, demonstrates that mobile technology is not just for traditional games. Through this location-based program, users can tell friends where they are by checking in to a place or event. Users of Foursquare earn points and virtual badges for these activities. They can even be appointed mayor of a place or event, translating into free products, foods, or other deals. Users have an incentive to keep earning points while businesses get publicity. The creators of Foursquare

Zynga's FarmVille became one of the world's most popular games because of its enticing reward system.

created a kind of digital reward punch card for businesses and gamified going out for a meal, shopping, or simply running errands for users.

The gamification of commerce through Foursquare is obvious. It fulfills two aspects of a successful game. There are achievable goals: checking in to a place or event a certain number of times. There are rewards: users receive badges as well as financial rewards. While there is no fantasy world, Foursquare gamifies nongame activities, making them more enjoyable. Twenty million people are members of Foursquare and about two billion check-ins are reported every day. Clearly, Foursquare offers motivation for users.

Though mobile devices are not a necessary part of gamifying an issue or activity, they have paved the way for more types of gamification. Most people carry their devices around and therefore a game is always within reach. The fervor for FarmVille and Foursquare has people using their mobile devices everywhere they go. Those using mobile technology for gamifying other issues hope to encounter as much success as these commercial gaming ventures.

Chapter 2

Gamifying the Environment

The three R's of green living are recycle, reuse, and reduce. Even preschoolers can recite these virtues. They learn how to help the environment and practice everyday actions that can make an impact on a community. However, early education does not mean that everyone puts in the extra effort to compost or walks a few more steps to recycle a can. Environmental issues are another area in which gamification can inject a bit of fun and motivation into some ordinary, though important, day-to-day activities.

Recyclebank

Recyclebank is a free online application through which users are rewarded for green activities. Recyclebank members earn points not only for recycling but also for such actions as unplugging appliances, choosing environmentally friendly products, using less water, carpooling, and taking public transportation. Points translate into discounts and gift cards from business partners of Recyclebank—about three thousand local and national companies.

Rewards such as these inspire people to make lifestyle changes or to just keep up the good work. An education component of Recyclebank includes online quizzes about ecology and energy. Members who complete them are said to "learn and earn" points. The platform is also a place for eco-conscious people to communicate and share information.

Recyclebank was an early adopter of gamification. Begun in New York City, it is now involved directly in three hundred communities in the United States and the United Kingdom and boasts more than four million online users. The majority of the company's revenue comes from its efforts to encourage people to recycle. In return for positive results, communities and waste companies pay Recyclebank a percentage of the money generated by recycling rather than taking trash to landfills.

Has Recyclebank made an impact? Cincinnati, Ohio, partnered with Recyclebank. The city reported impressive numbers after just a year of the rewards program, including a 49 percent increase in the amount of recycling (by weight) and a 75 percent increase in the number of recycling participants. This translates into the city saving approximately $1 million that would have gone to landfill costs.

Recyclebank offers users encouragement in their eco-friendly behaviors so that difficult goals seem achievable. Individuals can feel they are helping make a major impact.

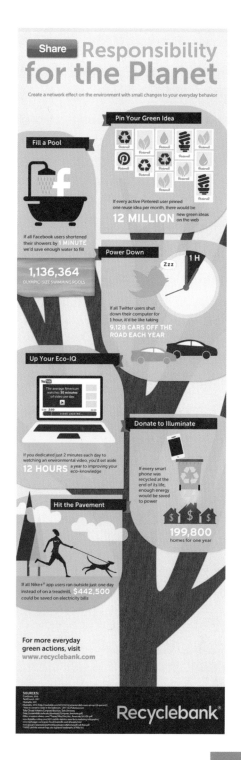

Zoo Game

The Gbanga company, in collaboration with the zoo of Zurich, Switzerland, released a storytelling application for cell phones and other Web-accessible devices called Gbanga Zooh. The zoo had two goals: attracting new people to the zoo and educating the public about the plight of endangered animals. Gbanga decided to "export" the zoo into the city of Zurich.

Most gaming applications are for individuals, so app developers rely on people to share their enthusiasm for products. Sometimes they offer incentives for users to get their friends to participate.

In the first part of the "mixed reality" game, users walked around Zurich and "picked up" virtual animals at certain sites. For example, they might go to the park in order to "catch" a tiger. The application was location-aware, so users had to be at certain places to fulfill that part of the quest.

When all of the animals were "captured," the user took his or her phone to the zoo for a reward—virtual seeds needed for the next part of the game. Players used the seeds to plant a healthy virtual environment for the endangered animals on their cell phone application. As they tended to the habitats, the animals thrived. If they neglected the habitats, the animals became sick.

File   Edit   View   Favorites   Tools   Help

SAP

SAP

Software company SAP has released several applications to help users track their carbon footprints. The Home Carbon Challenge is a Facebook application that tracks estimated or actual energy output in the home and makes suggestions about ways to reduce costs and energy use. Users can even challenge friends and neighbors to do the same.

One SAP application for businesses is called Vampire Hunter. The object of this game is to hunt for "vampires," another name for products that suck up energy unnecessarily. Employees take pictures of offending devices in the workplace, such as inefficient lightbulbs or unused equipment plugged in to a power source. The photos are sent to a "vampire headquarters" so that these energy wasters will be altered or unplugged. "Vampire hunters" are awarded with points according to the measurement of power saved from "killing the vampires." The business ultimately saves money on power bills.

The Gbanga Zooh platform was considered a success. It brought people into the zoo and taught them about the animals, their needs, and their habitats. The scavenger-hunt qualities of the first part of the game provided a dash of fantasy in real life. Part two of the application required a certain knowledge of conservation, fulfilling another goal of the zoo. The Gbanga Zooh application was a one-time campaign and its long-term impact is unknown.

The Fun Theory

The Volkswagen automobile company and the ad agency DDB Stockholm put together a campaign that proved how adding a fun element to ordinary activities can improve people's behaviors, even without the use of digital games. The campaign was in the form of videos, each depicting a kind of social experiment. In one ad, a video called "The World's Deepest Waste Bin," a noisemaker was installed in an ordinary trash can in a park. When someone dropped a piece of garbage into the can, the noisemaker made it sound like the trash fell for a long, long time. People lined up just to use the bin, which accumulated 159 pounds (72 kilograms) of trash in one day. The ordinary trash can next to it collected just 90 pounds (41 kg).

In another ad, a glass-recycling bin was converted into a "Bottle Bank Arcade." Blinking lights guided users as they put their bottles into certain holes at certain times. Accuracy and speed awarded each user with points, much like a real arcade game. Volkswagen reported that in one evening, the bottle bin collected bottles from one hundred people; just two people used the nearby bottle container.

Though these campaigns were successful in getting people to recycle and throw out their trash, would the activities lose their motivating and fun qualities if all trash cans and recycling bins had these features? Perhaps, but their initial success shows that there is merit in the ideas.

TEN GREAT QUESTIONS

TO ASK A GAME PRODUCER

1 What is the most enjoyable part of making a game?

2 What kinds of skills are needed to make a game?

3 What education do you need to learn how to make different kinds of games?

4 If I have a great idea for a game, how do I get in touch with someone to help me?

5 What is the most important element of a game?

6 What elements are missing from many unsuccessful games?

7 What are the steps in the process of making a game?

8 What are the similarities in developing a board game and a video game?

9 What are the biggest misconceptions that people have about games?

10 Do you have any advice for someone hoping to get into the gaming industry?

Chapter 3

Gamifying Education

Games and rewards have always been a reason for young people to do a job well, and schools have long been laboratories for gamification. Even as old an idea as a spelling bee gamifies the spelling lesson. It encourages learners to study to succeed, puts students on teams, and provides a reward, or at least recognition, to a winner.

In *Experience and Education*, early twentieth-century educational reformer John Dewey urged teachers to "utilize the surroundings, physical and social, that exist so as to extract from them all that they have to contribute to building up experiences that are worth while." Technology is now readily available in most schools. Computers, interactive whiteboards, and tablets are a permanent part of many classrooms. The only question is whether technology is used effectively to make the educational experience worthwhile. Gamification can add to this experience.

Classroom Gamification So Far

When some people think of gamifying education, they think of students playing so-called educational video games. Though some games are

Students play a game called *Restaurant Empire* to learn about the many sides of the restaurant industry.

helpful, especially with reinforcement, many fall short. Either they do not engage learners or they do not offer meaningful experiences. Sometimes these games are neither fun nor educational. According to researchers Mark Lepper and Diana Cordova's article in the journal *Motivation and Emotion,* "Learning goals have to be essential for winning [a game] or the material is likely to be ignored." They contend that a student learns more through the traditional methods of listening, memorizing, and practicing than through games without learning goals.

However, it is crucial not to give up on all aspects of games in the classroom. No one can deny that young people are drawn to them. Given the proper gaming experience, students are motivated to play and learn at home as well as at school. Video games also offer the opportunity of failure, which can be a positive learning experience. Gamers fail all the time, but they start over and amend their actions until they get it right. This could translate well in an educational game, whereas failure on a test or quiz can halt the learning process. Educators need to research games and match them to their students' needs.

A teacher at the Quest to Learn school in New York City examines students' DNA model, a gamification project reflecting the school's commitment to adding incentives to the curriculum.

Video games are just a small part of the gamification of education. What about actually gamifying the classroom experience? What if young students could monitor their progress on electronic tablets? Would they feel more in control? Could students in higher education be lured to attend class more if they "checked in" to their classroom? What if they could earn badges that factored into their grades, somewhat like a reward on Foursquare? These are just some of the ideas of future educators.

At least one school has bought in to the gamification concept completely. The Quest to Learn school in New York City offers classes for grades six through nine. While still meeting state-based learning standards, teachers incorporate games and game design into every part of the curriculum. In an interview with NPR, Katie Salen, an executive director, said, "The big idea of the school is we looked at how games work—literally how they're built and the way they support learning—and we thought we could design a school from the ground up that supported learning in the way games do." Salen and the other directors made that idea a reality. In one class, students role-play in "Creepytown," learning concepts of math and English. In another class, learners play specialized video games and even study game design to make their own games.

How does Quest to Learn compare to more traditional schools? According to the New York City Department of Education, the school received an overall rating of B. The school plans to eventually expand to grade twelve.

Young People as Game Makers

Recent game developers have been focusing on making games an integral part of a school lesson. They acknowledge the passivity of playing many video games. Often learners respond positively to moving around, interacting with others, and examining material in ways alternative to traditional techniques. Two organizations in particular are seeing success by giving learners the reins in a game's development.

File   Edit   View   Favorites   Tools   Help

GAMIFICATION IN THE U.S. DEPARTMENT OF EDUCATION

Gamification in the U.S. Department of Education

President Barack Obama and Secretary of Education Arne Duncan announced Race to the Top. In this points-based program, $4.35 billion in federal grants were awarded to states according to their visible signs of education reform. Each state application was worth a maximum total of five hundred points,

based on criteria such as teacher effectiveness and evidence of turnaround in low-achieving schools. States with the highest points received the largest portions of funding. First-place Tennessee was awarded $500 million, and Delaware won $100 million. Later, the contest was opened to school districts rather than states.

President Barack Obama and U.S. Secretary of Education Arne Duncan speak to middle-school students. Education officials continually search for ways to improve school performance.

Scratch

The Lifelong Kindergarten Group of the Massachusetts Institute of Technology's Media Lab developed Scratch, a free programming language for young people between eight and sixteen years old. Users can make their own animation, music, art, and games online and share them with others. They create games by dragging code fragments called blocks onto a certain area of a computer screen. Groups of blocks control aspects of the game, such as movements, visuals, and sounds.

Student-generated material takes learning to a higher level, especially if the games are meant to teach fellow classmates. The Lifelong Kindergarten Group calls this method of instruction "learning by designing." It gives students control and responsibility for the material. They are taken out of their traditional passive roles and assume the active roles of teachers. The young game designers must not only know what they want to teach but also how others will learn through their creations. Student Scratch projects can be made available for both teachers and other students to play and evaluate. Teachers can find out if students have learned key lesson concepts through their games and through their evaluations of others' games.

Scratch is inspired by two educational theories: constructivism and constructionism. Constructivist theory argues that people learn best from their own experiences. Constructionist theory states that people learn best when they are creating. In addition to being a platform for other curricula, Scratch introduces students to basic concepts of computer science and design theory. In the *New York Times*, Mitchel Resnick, head of the Scratch project, said, "It's like teaching them to write instead of only reading."

Kodu

Microsoft's Kodu is also a free programming language for young people. It is presented in a visual format for both personal computers and the Xbox 360 gaming system. Young people select icons from pop-up menus for their game. They choose scenes and populate them with the objects and characters they want. The designers also select rules concerning how characters and objects react.

To encourage young people to use Kodu and show off what the game design platform can do, Microsoft developed the Kodu Cup for ages nine to seventeen. The winning entries had narratives meant to educate players about issues. One winner created a game about combating pollution. Players had to plant trees and shut down factories. Another winner's game placed players in a world battling the aftereffects of a nuclear war.

Chapter 4

Gamifying Health

olkswagen's Fun Theory campaign included a fitness experiment. A stairway in a subway was turned into a working piano. The question: would people be more willing to use these stairs rather than use the nearby escalator and elevator? According to the report, 66 percent more people used the piano stairs than usual. Now at seventeen million views on YouTube, this video shows that an amusing idea can promote exercise in a community.

Fitness Apps and More

The consistently high ratings of the reality show *The Biggest Loser* demonstrate our culture's interest in wellness, specifically weight loss. Contestants compete to stay on the show. Weekly challenges and a season-ending prize make it compelling to millions. Could the game aspect of *The Biggest Loser* be applied to average people? It can and it has. Gamification is a natural fit in the area of wellness.

Two contestants on *The Biggest Loser* compete in a challenge. Participants are motivated by multiple rewards, both short-term and long-term.

Nike+

Many fitness applications are available to help people on their journey to a healthy lifestyle. Nike+ was one of the first. It tracks distance and pace. Runners and walkers attach a sensor to their sneakers, download the smartphone application, or use another compatible mobile device. Cost varies depending on the device and application.

If users program a goal into their digital device, they receive feedback. Celebrity athletes such as Tiger Woods offer recorded messages at milestones.

File   Edit   View   Favorites   Tools   Help

HEALTH INSURANCE JOINS THE GAME

Health Insurance Joins the Game

One of the major sponsors of health-related applications—and one that stands to profit from people's good health—is the health insurance industry. Blue Cross Blue Shield invested in a startup called EveryMove. This application awards members points for physical activity. In the early testing stages of the application, users who gathered a certain number of points were awarded gift certificates to health-related stores.

In a UnitedHealth survey, more than 50 percent of UnitedHealth customers reported that fitness games would encourage them to be more active. UnitedHealth responded by giving Xboxes and Microsoft's Kinect to obese young people. Kinect is a motion-sensing device that allows players to use their own body movements to control actions on the game screen.

People demonstrate Kinect at the Electronic Entertainment Expo. Users receive feedback about their performance and encouragement to keep moving.

After a workout, the device is synced to a computer so that personal statistics can be recorded and saved.

Charity Miles

Need more motivation for a workout than a virtual pat on the back? Charity Miles is a free application for the iPhone and Android phone. It uses a smartphone's GPS to track miles and times for walkers, runners, and cyclists. Users share their workouts on Facebook and Twitter. The twist is that each goal met equals a donation to a member's charity. Cyclists earn 10 cents per mile, while walkers and runners earn 25 cents per mile.

The Nike+ app with GPS capability tracks distance, pace, time, route, elevation, and calories burned. It also allows users to share information and challenge each other.

Currently, nine charities benefit from Charity Miles, including Autism Speaks, Feeding America, and Habitat for Humanity. The company behind the application contributed the first $1 million donated to athletes' charities. Its continued success is dependent on corporate sponsors' contributions.

GymPact

For many people, just getting to the gym is a problem. Two Harvard University students came up with the GymPact application to overcome self-imposed obstacles. Money is the reward and the punishment. GymPact users commit to a fitness schedule. They check in at a gym, and their presence is verified by their smartphone's GPS. However, if they do not meet their

File   Edit   View   Favorites   Tools   Help

GAMES FOR HEALTH

Games for Health

The Games for Health Project supports efforts to use games to improve health and health care. To date, Games for Health has brought together researchers, medical professionals, and game developers to share information about the impact that gamification can have on health issues. One major effort is the annual Games for Health Conference. Over the course of three days, more than four hundred attendees focus on topics including "exergaming," physical therapy, disease management, health behavior change, training, nutrition, and health education. While Games for Health does not provide funding for individual platforms, it helps connect interested parties.

GymPact is expanding its app beyond the gym to include runners, walkers, and cyclists who can be tracked by GPS.

schedule, money is deducted from their credit card accounts. At the end of a month, the money collected from members who missed their quotas is divided among those who met their goals.

According to a GymPact founder, about 90 percent of members are successful in meeting their goals. As further incentive, the more times users go to the gym, the more they earn. With current member-ship, members earn about 50 to 75 cents per workout.

Family of Heroes

Gamification does not just apply to physical health. Post-traumatic stress disor-der has been a concern for many returning soldiers trying to assimilate back into their normal lives. *Family of Heroes* is an online role-playing game for veterans and their families. The game helps players identify certain challenges and directs them to help when needed.

Avatars respond like real soldiers experiencing post-deployment stress, giving users hands-on practice in talking about problems in a safe, risk-free environment. The game was developed by a health and behavioral company called Kognito with the input of military families and the Veterans Affairs of New York and New Jersey. *Family of Heroes* is now available to more than 1.4 million veterans.

According to a study by the Games for Health Project, Family of Heroes has made an impact. Seven-nine percent of users identified an issue their veterans were dealing with and talked with them about their concern after playing the game. Twenty-two percent of veterans who were approached by a family member began to receive treatment for it. A whopping 98 percent of users rated the simulation as "very good" or "excellent" and would recommend it to others.

And Much More

The HealthRally social network lets users collect rewards from family and friends for positive actions, such as quitting smoking. HealthPrize rewards people for following their medication schedule. An inhaler-training device called the T-Haler teaches patients how to use an inhaler with the aid of a wireless device. According to the Cambridge Consultants company, T-Haler training increased patients' correct use of inhalers from 20 to 60 percent.

Clearly, the many issues of health can be gamified in many different ways. But not even popularity means that an application will be around in another five years. The Fitocracy fitness application and social network is a success with 450,000 members gained in just two years. However, it has a problem much like many others: the cost of running the business. Cofounder Brian Wang admits his business has no financial plan. On the Web site Xconomy.com, Wang said, "Revenue is not a huge focus right now. Our core strategy has to be about building a huge and awesome platform." Will advertising eventually cover the costs? Will sponsors step in? Will people value the application enough to pay? Only those platforms that prove their worth will likely survive.

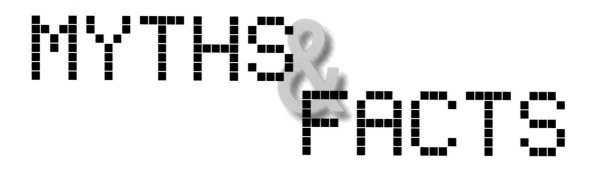

MYTHS & FACTS

MYTH Gamification is a new phenomenon.

FACT People have been using games to motivate people for a long time. Only the term "gamification" is new.

MYTH Gamification is a fad.

FACT Games are not a fad, so gamification is not likely to be a fad either. While not all ideas will work, others—such as Foursquare and Wii Fit—are proving to be successful and long-lasting.

MYTH Games are only for kids.

FACT The average gamer is about thirty-seven years old, so games are not just for kids anymore.

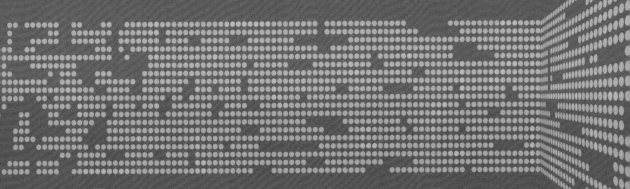

Chapter 5

Making a Worldwide Impact

Environmental, educational, and wellness issues have been gamified in some effective, surprising, and innovative ways. Perhaps there is no boundary for gamification. Games for Change is one of the biggest supporters of individuals and companies tackling unique social matters with gamification.

Social Impact Games

Games for Change, or G4C, is an organization that provides many services for those developing social impact games. G4C also helps nonprofit groups and others incorporate games into their online platforms to engage people. Games for Change clients include USAID, the World Bank Institute, the American Museum of Natural History, and CURE International. Games touch on a variety of topics, including humanitarianism, environmentalism, economics, human rights, and women's issues. For example, the National Endowment for the Arts granted G4C $75,000 for the adaptation of a

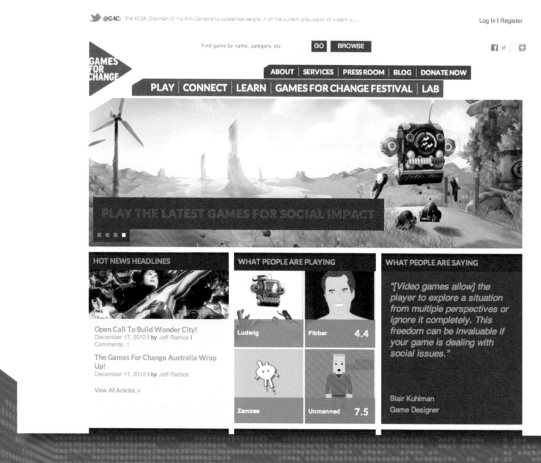

Check out the Games for Change Web site (www.gamesforchange.org) for the newest additions to its arcade. Games often reflect issues in the news.

book about oppressed African and Asian women called *Half the Sky* into a game for Facebook.

The Games for Change organization holds an annual festival as a showcase. Over eight hundred participants from governments, corporations, media, schools, and the game industry explore the implications of digital games as agents for social change. The initial success of G4C has led to chapters in Europe, Latin America, and Korea. The Games for Change Web site also has an online arcade where it hosts and provides links to many games.

Evoke

Games for Change gave a Direct Impact award to the game *Evoke*. The ten-week gaming "experience" involved players all over the world working together to solve problems that affect regions of Africa. As each week's events unfolded, players dug deeper into social issues and used prior knowledge and personal creativity to develop solutions to real-world problems. In addition to collaborating, players created individual blogs, videos, and photo galleries to share with the *Evoke* community. The game is free and supported financially by grants and nonprofit organizations, such as the World Bank.

Copresidents of Games for Change, Asi Burak and Michelle Byrd, speak about plans to collaborate with the Tribeca Film Institute to explore the merging of the gamification and filmmaking processes.

PeaceMaker

Another game featured on G4C's Web site is *PeaceMaker*. It is set in the Middle East, and users play the part of either the Israeli prime minister or the Palestinian president. They are presented with real-world events in the form of headlines and news footage. The goal is to establish peace and win the Nobel Peace Prize, even as events escalate into violence. *PeaceMaker*'s developers hope to challenge perspectives and misconceptions about the Israeli/Palestinian conflict. The game can be played in English, Hebrew, or Arabic.

Games in Science and Medicine

Firas Khatib, a researcher at the University of Washington, offered a puzzle to the public that had stumped scientists for years. Khatib had been trying to figure out the structure of a specific protein tangled in a protein group. This protein is found in monkeys suffering from a virus similar to AIDS. In an effort to stop the virus, scientists needed to know how the single protein was constructed.

Khatib recruited gamers to find the structure of the protein using an online multi-player program called *Foldit*. *Foldit* allows users to figure out three-dimensional shapes with easy controls. Users are scored based on the stability of the structure they end up with. High scores are ranked on a leader board. Users chat in online forums, work in groups to solve puzzles, and share solutions, too. Most of Khatib's recruits were not scientists and did not have a background in science. They simply liked a puzzle. Khatib's gamers took just three weeks to find the structure of the protein. In *Discover* magazine online, Khatib said, "This is the first instance that we are aware of in which online gamers solved a longstanding scientific problem. These results indicate the potential for integrating video games into the real-world scientific process: the ingenuity of game players is a formidable force."

Sepsis, a condition caused by the presence of toxins in tissue or the bloodstream, is a major problem in hospitals today. According to the online *Critical Care* medical journal, about 750,000 people contract sepsis each

File   Edit   View   Favorites   Tools   Help

◁   ▷   ↻   ⌂   GAMING'S POSITIVE EFFECTS ON THE AGING

Gaming's Positive Effects on the Aging

Gaming has been shown to boost cognitive activity in the elderly. A University of Illinois study instructed a group of elderly people to play a strategic video game called *Rise of Nations*. After just a day, the group saw improvements in multitasking, concentration, and short-term memory when compared to a control group that did not participate. In addition to mental wellness, systems such as Wii Fit and Kinect may help with physical fitness in nursing homes and assisted-living facilities.

year, with about 215,000 fatalities. The Stanford University of Medicine developed the Septris application to help doctors better identify sepsis in their patients.

In Septris, doctors tend to the needs of virtual patients. They can see medical histories, lab results, and more. They recommend treatments and watch as their patients either get better or worse. Quizzes and tips reinforce concepts. Septris can be downloaded to a mobile device or used on a personal computer. The developers believe it will be more effective than lecture-based continuing education classes and that its "addictive" qualities will motivate doctors to continue playing—and learning.

The Future of Gamification

While there is seemingly no limit to the issues that can be gamified, there are limitations to whether the game can help users achieve goals. Simply making a game does not guarantee its success in the long run, even if it has immediate appeal. People must continue playing until the goal is achieved. The concept of users staying with a program is called "stickiness." The more

The future success of the gamification movement depends on attracting the interest of those who would not usually play games. Developers must continue to tap into the needs of the public.

the game includes the traits of a successful game—goals, interest, and rewards—the more likely it will be sticky. To truly impact a social issue, the game must engage the user in a meaningful, motivating experience.

There are still many skeptical of gamification because they are skeptical of games. They think of video games as a solitary escape from reality. However, the gamification movement is providing experiences that are the opposite. A well-made social impact gaming experience can inspire people to band together to tackle real-world issues. Perhaps not every game will have the same effect on every person, but many have already changed lives.

arcade An area where people can play video games or other game machines.

assimilate To enter into a larger group so that differences become minimized.

avatar A three-dimensional image that can be used to represent somebody in cyberspace.

carbon footprint The amount of greenhouse gases, specifically carbon dioxide, emitted by a person's activities during a given period.

cognitive Relating to the process of acquiring knowledge by using reasoning.

conservation The preservation, management, and care of natural resources.

criteria Accepted standards used in making decisions or judgments.

curricula The range of subjects that are taught by a particular school district.

deployment The act of sending troops, weapons, and resources to an area in readiness for action.

incentive Something that encourages or motivates somebody to do something.

ingenuity Cleverness and originality.

passivity The quality of not being active.

post-traumatic stress disorder A condition that may affect people who have suffered great emotional stress.

programming The designing or writing of computer programs.

quota A maximum number or quantity needed.

revenue Money that comes into a business from the sale of goods or services.

simulation A reproduction of something to aid in study or training.

sync In computers, it is an abbreviation for "synchronize." It means to compare at least two sets of data and make them match each other.

Ayogo Games
314 West Cordova Street #210
Vancouver, BC V6B 1E8
Canada
(888) 680-9882
Web site: http://ayogo.com
This Canadian game development company focuses on "games for good" that educate and motivate people.

Bunchball
2200 Bridge Parkway, Suite 201
Redwood City, CA 94065
(408) 985-2034
Web site: http://www.bunchball.com
Bunchball is one of the leading companies integrating gamification into the workplace.

Games for Change
78 Fifth Avenue, 5th Floor
New York, NY 10011
(212) 242-4922
Web site: http://www.gamesforchange.org
Games for Change is the global advocate for social impact games encompassing a variety of issues.

Games for Health Project
P.O. Box 17575
Portland, ME 04101
(207) 773-3700

Web site: http://www.gamesforhealth.org
The Games for Health Project promotes gamification in an effort to improve
    wellness and health care.

Project Whitecard, Inc.
200-135 Innovation Drive
Winnipeg, MN R3T 6A8
Canada
(855) 269-0718
Web site: http://www.projectwhitecard.com
This is a Canadian game developer picked by NASA to create an online
    game about space colonization.

Quest to Learn
351 West 18th Street, 4th Floor
New York, NY 10011
(212) 488-3645
Web site: http://www.q2l.org
Learn more about this school where curricula is taught using gamelike tech-
    niques and experiences.

Web Sites

Due to the changing nature of Internet links, Rosen Publishing has developed
an online list of Web sites related to the subject of this book. This site is
updated regularly. Please use this link to access the list:

http://www.rosenlinks.com/DIL/Game

FOR FURTHER READING

Chatfield, Tom. *Fun Inc.: Why Gaming Will Dominate the Twenty-First Century*. Trenton, TX: Pegasus, 2010.

Collins, Allan, and Richard Halverson. *Rethinking Education in the Age of Technology: The Digital Revolution and Schooling in America*. New York, NY: Teachers College Press, 2009.

Hunter, Robert. *The Gamification Handbook: Everything You Need to Know About Gamification*. Brisbane, Australia: Emereo Publishing, 2011.

Kapp, Karl. *The Gamification of Learning and Instruction: Game-Based Methods and Strategies for Training and Education*. San Francisco, CA: Pfeiffer, 2012.

McGonigal, Jane. *Reality Is Broken: Why Games Make Us Better and How They Can Change the World*. New York, NY: Penguin Press, 2011.

Michael, David, and Sande Chen. *Serious Games: Games That Educate, Train, and Inform*. Boston, MA: Thomson Course Technology PTR, 2006.

Squire, Kurt, and Henry Jenkins. *Video Games and Learning: Teaching and Participatory Culture in the Digital Age*. New York, NY: Teachers College Press, 2011.

Watkins, S. Craig. *The Young and the Digital: What the Migration to Social-Network Sites, Games, and Anytime, Anywhere Media Means for Our Future*. Boston, MA: Beacon Press, 2009.

Zackariasson, Peter, and Timothy L. Wilson. *The Video Game Industry: Formation, Present State, and Future*. New York, NY: Routledge, 2012.

Zichermann, Gabe, and Joselin Linder. *Game-Based Marketing: Inspire Customer Loyalty Through Rewards, Challenges, and Contests*. Hoboken, NJ: John Wiley & Sons, 2010.

BIBLIOGRAPHY

Albright, Glenn, Ron Goldman, Kristen M. Shockley, Fiona McDevitt, and
     Sam Akbas. "Games for Health, Research, Development and Clinical
     Applications," *Games for Health Journal*, Vol. 1, Issue 1, 2012.

Bernard, Tara Siegel. "GymPact Fines You for Not Exercising." January 2,
     2012. Retrieved June 25, 2012 (http://bucks.blogs.nytimes.com/2012
     /01/02/gym-pact-fines-you-for-not-exercising).

Cashmore, Pete. "The Fun Theory: Volkswagen Masters the Viral Video."
     Mashable.com, October 11, 2009. Retrieved June 15, 2012 (http://
     mashable.com/2009/10/11/the-fun-theory).

Chaplin, Heather. "School Uses Video Games to Teach Thinking Skills."
     NPR.org, June 28, 2010. Retrieved June 27, 2012 (http://www.npr
     .org/templates/story/story.php?storyId=128081896).

Corcoran, Elizabeth. "The 'Gamification' of Education." Forbes.com,
     October 29, 2010. Retrieved July 10, 2012 (http://www.forbes
     .com/2010/10/28/education-internet-scratch-technology-gamification
     .html?boxes=Homepagechannels).

Cross, Tim. "All the World's a Game." Economist.com, December 10,
     2011. Retrieved June 10, 2012 (http://www.economist.com/node
     /21541164).

Dewey, John. "Experience and Education." Retrieved July 12, 2012 (http://ruby
     .fgcu.edu/Courses/ndemers/Colloquium/ExperiencEducationDewey.pdf).

Fox, Zoe. "How One Startup Gamifies Recycling for a Greener World."
     Mashable.com, March 27, 2012. Retrieved July 1, 2012 (http://
     mashable.com/2012/03/27/recyclebank).

Gbanga. "About Gbanga." Gbanga.com. Retrieved May 26, 2012
     (http://gbanga.com/about).

Gunpoint. "What Makes Games Good." Pentadact.com. Retrieved June 30,
     2012 (http://www.pentadact.com/2011-05-27-what-makes-games
     -good).

Kolodny, Lora. "Recyclebank's CEO Jonathan Hsu on New Site, Rewarding Green Behavior Beyond the Bin." Techcrunch.com, February 1, 2011. Retrieved May 10, 2012 (http://techcrunch.com/2011/02/01/recyclebank-ceo-hsu-on-site-redesig).

Lawton, Chuck. "Winners Announced in the Kid-Centric Microsoft Kodu Cup." *Wired*, June 14, 2011. Retrieved June 24, 2012 (http://www.wired.com/geekdad/2011/06/winners-announced-in-the-kid-centric-microsoft-kodu-cup).

Lepper, Mark R., and Diana I. Codova. "A Desire to Be Taught: Instructional Consequences of Intrinsic Motivation." *Motivation and Emotion*, Vol. 16, No. 3, 1992, pp. 187–208.

Starting Point. "What Makes a Good Game?" Serc.carleton.edu. Retrieved July 2, 2012 (http://serc.carleton.edu/introgeo/games/goodgame.html).

Starting Point. "Why Use Games to Teach?" Serc.carleton.edu. Retrieved July 2, 2012 (http://serc.carleton.edu/introgeo/games/whygames.html).

U.S. Department of Education. "Race to the Top Fund." Ed.gov. Retrieved July 2, 2012 (http://www2.ed.gov/programs/racetothetop/index.html).

Woods, Dan. "Gamification Grows Up to Become a CEO's Best Friend." Forbes.com, May 14, 2012. Retrieved July 1, 2012 (http://www.forbes.com/sites/danwoods/2012/05/14/gamification-grows-up-to-become-a-ceos-best-friend).

Yong, Ed. "Computer Gamers Solve Problem in AIDS Research That Puzzled Scientists for Years." DiscoverMagazine.com, September 18, 2011. Retrieved June 20, 2012 (http://blogs.discovermagazine.com/notrocketscience/2011/09/18/computer-gamers-solve-problem-in-aids-research-that-puzzled-scientists-for-years).

INDEX

About the Author

Therese Shea, an author and former educator, has written over one hundred books on a wide variety of subjects. Her most recent have delved into topics of technology including robotics, cyberbullying, and a biography of Apple cofounder Steve Jobs. She holds degrees from Providence College and the State University of New York at Buffalo. The author currently resides in Atlanta, Georgia, with her husband, Mark.

Photo Credits

Cover and p. 1 (from left) Andresr/Shutterstock.com, bannosuke/Shutterstock.com, Robert Kneschke/Shutterstock.com, ollyy/Shutterstock.com; p. 5 Yellow Dog Productions/The Image Bank/Getty Images; p. 8 Aleksandr Markin/Shutterstock.com; p. 9 iStockphoto/Thinkstock; p. 11 David Livingston/WireImage/Getty Images; p. 12 Zynga/AP Images; p. 15 PR Newswire/AP Images; p. 16 Riccardo Piccinini/Shutterstock.com; pp. 21, 28 © AP Images; p. 22 Chicago Tribune/McClatchy-Tribune/Getty Images; p. 24 Saul Loeb/AFP/Getty Images; p. 29 Michal Czerwonka/Getty Images; p. 30 © iStockphoto.com/Roman Ponomarets; p. 32 Jamie Grill/Iconica/Getty Images; p. 36 Courtesy of Games for Change; p. 37 Jemal Countess/Getty Images; p. 40 PhotoAlto/Frederic Cirou/Getty Images; cover (background) and interior page graphics © iStockphoto.com/suprun.

Designer: Nicole Russo; Editor: Nicholas Croce; Photo Researcher: Karen Huang